Dedication

This book is dedicated to my mother Marlys.
She inspired me to write
'Marsie The Littlest Majorette'
Thank you for reading to me so often.
You inspire me to create & to be prolific.

I0827888

Kidlink Inc.'s

MY SUPER DUPER STORYBOOK OF AWESOME BIG ADVENTURES! VOLUME #3

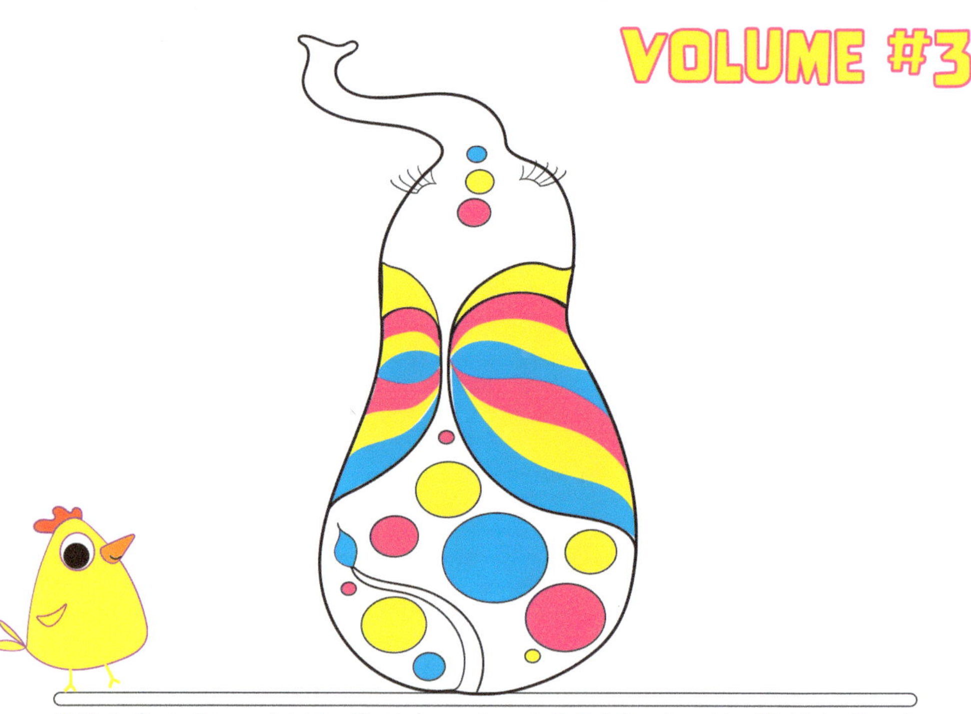

Kidlink, Inc. Supports the First Amendment & Celebrates the Right to Read.

Written & Illustrated by Beth Lynn Danielson
Photographs by Beth Lynn Danielson

Author: Beth Lynn Danielson
My Super Duper Storybook of Awesome Big Adventures Volume 3
For information about special discounts on bulk purchases, please contact Kidlink, Inc. Special Sales at gokidlink@gmail.com

ISBN: 978-1-7338455-5-7

THIS BOOK BELONGS TO:

Circus Super Duper!

The polka dot elephant likes to take a giant bubble bath.
She always giggles merrily & makes the monkeys laugh.
Monkey Wunkey plays a tune on the accordion.
The melody is fabulous! It pleases the Mr. Morgan.
Lucky the Lion leaps upon the circus balls & then
When the show is over he leaps right back again.
Winnie the Walrus always has a song to sing so fine.
When her voice booms through the tent the folks just jump in line.
Square Bear always dances a jig underneath the lights.
Sometimes he will wear his clogs & tap them with delight!
Tommy Turtle has a funny juggling act to do.
He doesn't really juggle, it just looks like that (with glue)
Gogo is hilarious when he jumps in the ring!
He can run so fast and make the bells go "Ding, ding, ding!"
The Polar Bear Parade is such an awesome sight to see.
Bingo leads the way! He is the Birthday Bear! Yippee!
Shimmer Seal is elegant & glitters in the dark.
She is so fantastic when she whistles, claps & barks!
Rainbow the Unicorn is next in the 'Big Show'!
She can canter smoothly & her rainbow mane will flow.
Zippy Zebra loves the show. His stripes are fabulous!
He leads the dancing bears onto the train without a fuss.
Astro the Kodiak is as blue as he can be.
Once upon a winter day his fur just froze frosty!
The Super Stinkers always jump into the ring on time.
"Welcome to the Circus Super Duper!" they both chime!
So when you want excitement cuz your day is needing fun,
Watch 'Circus Super Duper'! You will love it! It's the ONE!

Baby Bamboo

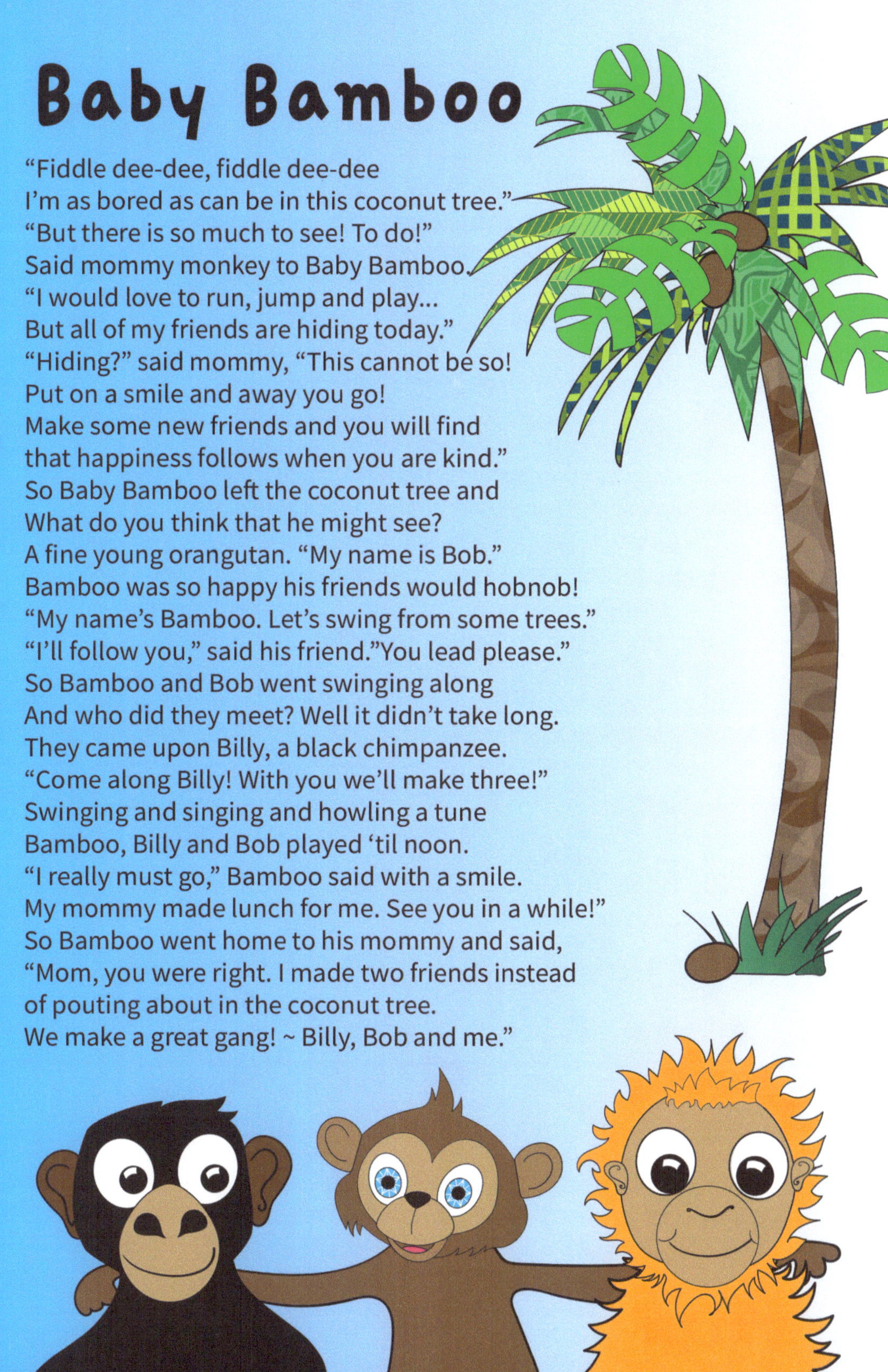

"Fiddle dee-dee, fiddle dee-dee
I'm as bored as can be in this coconut tree."
"But there is so much to see! To do!"
Said mommy monkey to Baby Bamboo.
"I would love to run, jump and play...
But all of my friends are hiding today."
"Hiding?" said mommy, "This cannot be so!
Put on a smile and away you go!
Make some new friends and you will find
that happiness follows when you are kind."
So Baby Bamboo left the coconut tree and
What do you think that he might see?
A fine young orangutan. "My name is Bob."
Bamboo was so happy his friends would hobnob!
"My name's Bamboo. Let's swing from some trees."
"I'll follow you," said his friend."You lead please."
So Bamboo and Bob went swinging along
And who did they meet? Well it didn't take long.
They came upon Billy, a black chimpanzee.
"Come along Billy! With you we'll make three!"
Swinging and singing and howling a tune
Bamboo, Billy and Bob played 'til noon.
"I really must go," Bamboo said with a smile.
My mommy made lunch for me. See you in a while!"
So Bamboo went home to his mommy and said,
"Mom, you were right. I made two friends instead
of pouting about in the coconut tree.
We make a great gang! ~ Billy, Bob and me."

Happy, Happy, Happy!

When I see our spotted cow what I like to do
Is share my corn with her and then she makes a happy 'Moo!'
When I see our horse with his fuzzy winter coat
I fill a tiny bucket full of fine, fresh oats.
When I see the chickens clucking in their pen
I share bananas with them. They could eat ten!
When I see our grunting pig standing in the field,
I share some cookies with him and boy does he squeel!
When I see the ducklings swimming in the lake,
I share my bread crumbs with them cuz they can't bake.
When I see my goldfish swimming in his bowl,
I give him just two tiny flakes to satisfy his soul.
When I see my kitty cat purring like they do,
I give her bits of kibble then she mews a happy mew!
When I see my begging dog staring right at me,
I give him several bites of food and then he barks at me!
I love all the animals just the way they 'er .
All the critters love me too; feathers, scales or fur.
So when you see a critter who needs a bite or two,
Simply share your lunch with them. It's what I like to do.
They will thank you kindly by running fast and free.
Happy, Happy, Happy is how they like to be!

Little Quacker

There was a little duck who quacked all day.
He never listened to what others had to say.
His very best friend was a shy, brown squirrel.
Who never said a thing though his wisdom was like pearls.
The silly little duck just went on and on and on.
Squirrel was polite and listened 'til the sun was gone.
Little duck finally thought he'd better get some sleep.
Squirrel ran home quickly with some nuts that he would keep.
While little duck was lying in his bed that night he thought,
"I cannot remember what my friend squirrel said or not."
"I cannot remember if he said what I should do."
"I cannot remember if he said one thing or two."
"I had better listen up if I am going to be...
a better friend to my friend squirrel so he'll stay friends with me."
The next day little duck went on his way to see his friend.
"I am sorry squirrel. I didn't mean to talk 'til the day's end.
I promise that I'll listen to the things you have to say."
"It's alright duck," said shy, brown squirrel, "Let's go play!"

ON TOP OF THE WORLD!

I'm on top of the world!
Can you see? All the stuff that's under me?
My tummy, my legs, my feet & toes!
And this is how my story goes.
All the stuff that's under me
Means I'm on top of the world you see?
The rug, the dirt, the wooden floor...
And under that there's even more!
The boards, the plumbing of this big house...
Spiders, flies & even a mouse!
He lives in the basement & he agrees
That I'm on top of the world! Yes Me!
Free to play outside in the sun!
On top of the world & having fun!
There's even more stuff under all that...
Like all the layers of dirt that sat
For millions of years so don't you see?
I'm on top of the world! Just look at me!
The layers of rock that lay below
Right down to the core of the earth they go.
So I'm as happy as I can be!
On top of the world!! Tee Hee, Tee Hee! :)

★THE POLAR BEAR PARADE..

Polar Bears are somethin' else! They're big & white & bold.
They live out on the snow & ice.The live where it is cold.
You may not believe what I'm about to tell you though,
I heard it from Nanouk who is a native Eskimo.
Each year on the coldest night the starts light up the sky
The polar bears all gather, but not for apple pie.
They all hold hands together all wild & unafraid.
Standing proudly on the earth in a polar bear parade.

Flower Power

"Sugar Horse"

There once was a sugar white horse
Her name was Sugar of course
She was sweet as she could be
The children rode her merrily
5 at once on her back they'd climb
They had such a splendid time
Walking about the grass so green
Sugar was pretty as a figurine

The Polka Dot Elephant

The Polka Dot Elephant is sweet as can be
She won't interrupt or spill lavendar tea
She always remembers to ask how you are
And late every night she watches the stars
The Polka Dot Elephant has one fine friend
A small yellow bird on whom she can depend
They travel together on journeys afar
And always sing sweet songs together
... Hoo-rar!

Marsie The Littlest Majorette

Marsie led the big parade in Linton, her hometown
She wore a fine white hat & outfit sewn by her own mom
She taught herself to twirl baton & did it with such style
That people came from miles away (reports her brother Lyle)
"Look at her twirl!" the folks exclaimed as Marsie passed them by
She threw her baton in the air with a twinkle in her eye
"I can't believe that tiny girl can lead this big parade!"
Marsie was a wonder & completely unafraid
She showed those town folk how to march & twirl a smart baton
And you should know that Marsie was the town's phenomenon!

The Mermaid Parade

All the lovely mermaids of the deep & shining sea
Laugh & play & sing sweet songs while swimming merrily
In the morning they will wake & think about their day
After breakfast they will race outside to swim & play
All the tiny mermaids then will gather in a group
Lacing bubbles into strings & making shimmery loops
Racing by on silver sea horse ponies they will send
Splashes & sweet songs while riding waves with sunshine friends
So if you see the mermaids all lined up & riding waves
You have seen the magic of a sweet mermaid parade

Shimmer The Seal

Shimmer the seal can balance on a big round circus ball.
She also puts one on her nose and she will never fall.
She has the perfect balance as anyone can see.
Shimmer loves to show off all the time for you and me!

"Give It A BLAST!"

"Hey Boss, we can't build the highway cuz a Mountain is in the way."

"Give it a BLAST! Use some dynamite."

"Hey Boss, we can't make a copy cuz the copier's on fire."

"Give it a BLAST! Use the fire extinguisher."

"Hey Boss, there's a gopher in the irrigation pipe & he won't come out."

"Give it a BLAST! Turn on the pump."

"Hey Boss, your coffee is cold."

"Give it a BLAST! Use the microwave."

PORKITO BANDITO!

PORKITO BANDITO IS REALLY QUITE A GUY
HE LIKES TO EAT A SANDWICH AND HE'S NOT VERY SHY
HE WEARS A SLEEK BLACK MASK AND TRAVELS INCOGNITO
SO NO ONE IDENTIFIES GREAT PORKITO BANDITO
HE DEALS OUT JUSTICE WITH HIS MARSHMALLOW GUN
HE NEVER USES BULLETS CUZ HE'S IN IT JUST FOR FUN
SO IF YOU HAVE A NEED TO STRAIGHTEN OUT A CROOK
LOOK NO FURTHER THAN THE VERY PAGES OF THIS BOOK
HE WILL COME A HUNTING AND BE WITH YOU WHEN YOU GO
TO SHOOT THE CROOK WITH MARSHMALLOWS AND SHOUT OUT "PORKITO!"

Lemon Drop was a fat little pig.
She started life not very big.
But then she grew & grew & GREW!
She was HUGE before anyone knew!
One day at the County Fair,
While the judges were sitting there
A ribbon fair & very blue
Was given, well, to you know who!
Lemon Drop the finest pig!
Who started life not very big :)

“Humpty’s Space Mishap”

Humpty had chosen a lofty place
adrift on the moon in the limelight of space
“here,” he said proudly, “I simply can’t fall!
For here there is not even dust or a wall.”
Spinning around & around on his chin,
feeling important he wore a wide grin.
‘Til one day a cow flying by nicked his head.
”What a headache I have!” Poor old humpty said.
All those at Nasa & Spacex now too
Bobbed around humpty not knowing what to do.
Until one bright astronaut said “Reverse time!”
So that’s what they did & now Humpty’s prime.

The Whisker Fairy

The Whisker Fairy waves her wand
To give you whiskers... you'll be fond
Of fuzzy whiskers in a place
Where you had none upon your face
Whiskers here & Whiskers there
Fuzzy Whiskers everywhere!
1, 2, 3, 4, 5, 6, 7... 
It is simply Whisker Heaven! 
The Whisker Fairy's day is done
It's been quite nice...Yes it was fun
Tomorrow there is lots to do
She might have whiskers just for you!

Mouse Circus

The fabulous 'Mouse Circus' is a sight for all to see
Tiny is the Ringmaster; the leader of the three
Teenie is the fairy on trapeze which she does swing
Whiney is the baby and he makes 3 crickets sing
They always like performing for a happy little crowd
Tiny introduces acts and the crickets sing so loud
Teenie has a set of fairy wings translucent blue
The fabulous 'Mouse Circus' is terrific! It is true

MONKEE WUNKEE

Munkee Wunkee is a real fantastic little guy!
He plays the accordion with a twinkle in his eye.
He can wear a red cap and a coat as you can see.
Hopping to and fro and playing songs for you and me.
Monkee Wunkee likes to be in all the big parades.
He will sneak a piece of candy that the baker made.
When the fun is over and it's time to go to bed,
Monkee Wunkee brushes his white teeth with his friend Fred.

THE DANCING BEARS

The dancing bears are here!
The dancing bears are great!
They dance & ride their bicycles
And we won't have to wait!
They're really, really here!
It's super fun to see!
The dancing bears can roller skate
around for you and me!

The Poodle Parade

The poodle parade is fine as can be.
They all are dancing merrily.
They prance and hop and skitter about.
They jump through hoops~first in, then out.
They roll and hop and catch a toy.
The poodles are definitely filled with joy!
So come and see the fun we made
with our super fabulous poodle parade!

GOGO!

I had a little doggie and Gogo was his name.
He always fetched his favorite toy. Each day it was the same.
He licked my nose and wiggled when we went outside to play.
We had the greatest time together every single day!

Super Stinkers!

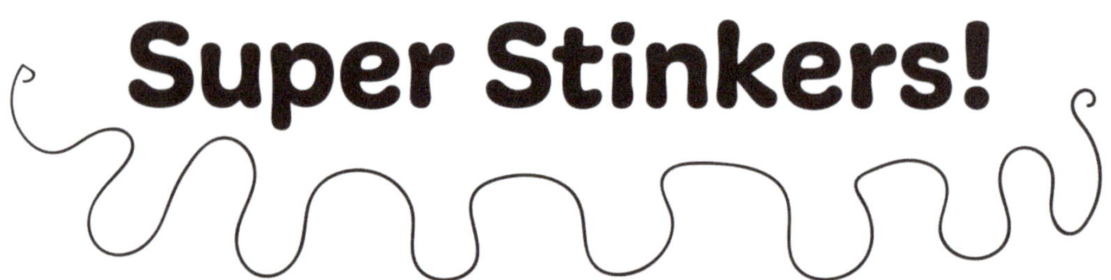

Oh yes we are the super stinkers my brother here and me!
We always are together and it's how we like to be!
We are the super stinkers! We're never far from home.
We always are together so we never are alone!

Bingo!

**My name is Bingo cuz I really love bingo.
Yes I'll play bingo wherever I can go to play some bingo
Cuz I love bingo! Yes I am Bingo the Birthday Bear!**

Little Pig, Little Pig

"Little pig, little pig... how do you do?"
"I am amazing. How are you?"
"Little pig, little pig... having dinner today?"
"Yes I am. Now go away."
"Little pig, little pig... I want some food too."
"That's interesting. Who invited you?"
"Little pig, little pig... I brought some cheese."
"Well what took you so long? Get in here!"

Piggly, Wiggly & Oink

Once upon a time there were three little pigs named Piggly, Wiggly & Oink. They danced around & hopped about & when they jumped they went 'Boink!' They loved to eat & run in the woods picking flowers on their way, but their very favorite thing to do was to wallow in mud & play. When Piggly woke up, Oink did too but Wiggly wanted to stay lazing in bed like a bad little pig... laziness was just his way. "Wiggle your tail & get out of bed!" his little brothers would say. But Wiggly just laid there & let out a grunt, lazily wasting the day. Until it just happened, that life changing thing, that Wiggly would never forget. An ant came along & crawled up his nose. That REALLY tickled I bet! So now when the brothers wake up to go play, Wiggly gets up with a start. Remember that laziness simply won't pay so get going & just do your part!

Pretty Pink Parrots

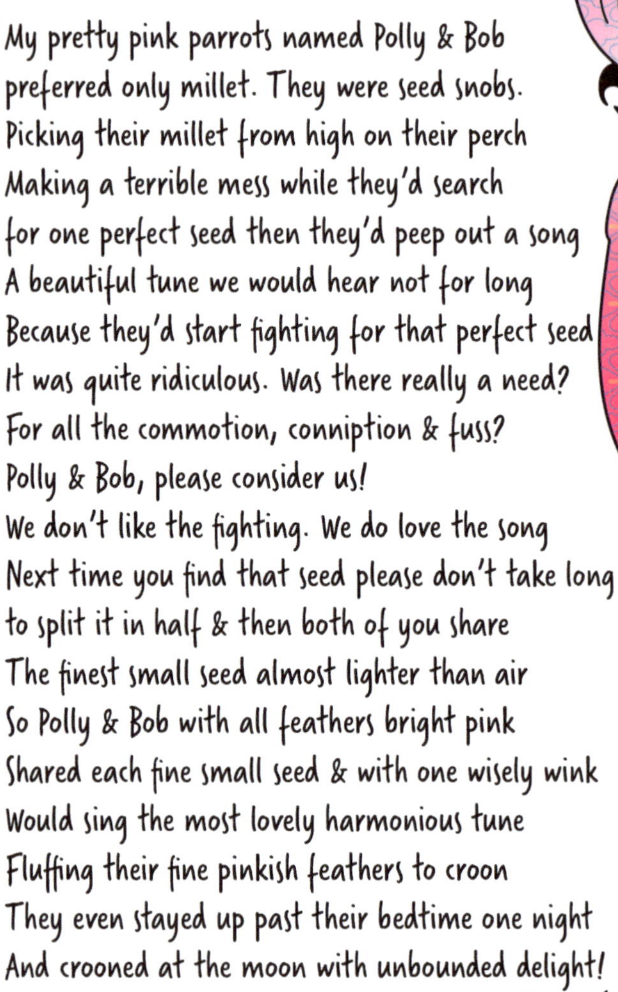

My pretty pink parrots named Polly & Bob
preferred only millet. They were seed snobs.
Picking their millet from high on their perch
Making a terrible mess while they'd search
for one perfect seed then they'd peep out a song
A beautiful tune we would hear not for long
Because they'd start fighting for that perfect seed
It was quite ridiculous. Was there really a need?
For all the commotion, conniption & fuss?
Polly & Bob, please consider us!
We don't like the fighting. We do love the song
Next time you find that seed please don't take long
to split it in half & then both of you share
The finest small seed almost lighter than air
So Polly & Bob with all feathers bright pink
Shared each fine small seed & with one wisely wink
Would sing the most lovely harmonious tune
Fluffing their fine pinkish feathers to croon
They even stayed up past their bedtime one night
And crooned at the moon with unbounded delight!

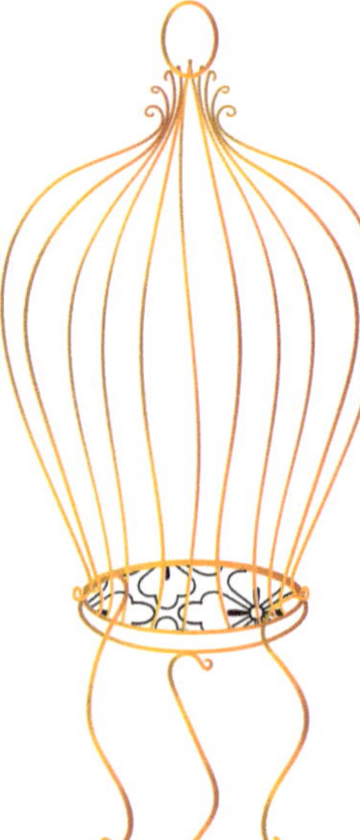

www.ingramcontent.com/pod-product-compliance
Lightning Source LLC
LaVergne TN
LVHW052303100826
845147LV00001B/124
* 9 7 8 1 7 3 3 8 4 5 5 5 7 *